SCIENCE GOES BOOM

Get ready to have a BLAST! This book and kit comes with 18 dynamite experiments that POP, FIZZ, and EXPLODE with noise, fun, and science!

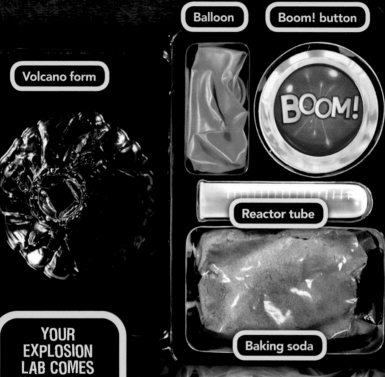

Balloon

Boom! button

Volcano form

BOOM!

Reactor tube

Baking soda

YOUR EXPLOSION LAB COMES WITH THESE COOL TOOLS!

⚠️

PLAY IT SAFE

Warning: DO NOT put hot liquids in the reactor tube!

SAFETY FIRST!

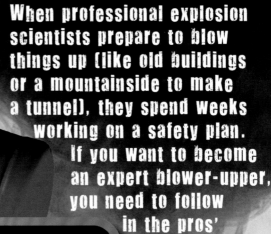

When professional explosion scientists prepare to blow things up (like old buildings or a mountainside to make a tunnel), they spend weeks working on a safety plan. If you want to become an expert blower-upper, you need to follow in the pros' footsteps.

Read these important safety tips. Then stick to them!

- Follow each experiment's instructions carefully. Changing the experiments' steps could be dangerous! Don't try to make up experiments or use materials other than those listed. Some common household chemicals can produce harmful vapors if they are mixed together.

- Make sure the lab area is clear of things that could break or be stained.

- Never point the open end of the reactor tube toward your face or toward anybody else.

- Don't eat or drink the results of your experiments.

- Know when to ask for help. If the instructions say you need an adult helper, **GET ONE ASAP!**

Written by Cody Crane and Kris Hirschmann

Illustrated by Daniel Jankowski
Designed by Ali Castro and Daniel Jankowski
Cover and package design by Ali Castro

Copyright© 2014 Scholastic Inc.

Scholastic and Tangerine Press and associated logos
are trademarks of Scholastic Inc.

Published by Tangerine Press, an imprint of Scholastic Inc.,
557 Broadway, New York, NY 10012

10 9 8 7 6 5 4 3 2 1

ISBN: 978-0-545-80799-9

Printed and bound in Shenzhen, China

an imprint of
■SCHOLASTIC
www.scholastic.com

TABLE OF CONTENTS

MEASUREMENTS

c = cups	**tbsp** = tablespoon
mi. = miles	**tsp** = teaspoon
m = meters	**ml** = milliliters
km = kilometers	**in.** = inches
mph = miles per hour	**cm** = centimeters
kph = kilometers per hour	**mm** = millimeters

Here are a few more tips to make sure your experiments go off without a hitch.

- Some of these experiments are MESSY. Get the OK from a parent before you start!

- If possible, work on a countertop near the kitchen sink, and completely cover your work area with newspaper.

- Some experiments are so messy that they are best done OUTSIDE. You might also consider wearing an old T-shirt that is okay to get RUINED.

- When you're done with an experiment, flush liquids down the drain. Put any solid or semi-solid materials in a plastic bag and toss them into the TRASH.

- Clean up your equipment after each experiment. If your equipment is DIRTY, your next experiment might not work.

SPECIAL CLEANING INSTRUCTIONS:

Reactor tube: Hand wash with lukewarm (not hot), soapy water and rinse well. **DO NOT** put it in the dishwasher.

EXPLOSIONS 101

You've probably seen colorful fireworks burst. What about an old building being demolished or a rocket launched into space? If so, then you've witnessed some real-life explosions in action.

It's not just human-made things that explode. Volcanoes, for example, have plenty of natural firepower. When they erupt, they can spew hot lava and shoot rocks the size of small cars into the air!

These are just a few examples of explosions. Let's learn a little bit about the science behind them.

EXPLOSIONS 101

WHAT IS AN EXPLOSION?

To answer this question, let's start with the scientific definition: An explosion is a rapid expansion that causes a violent release of energy. There are two main points in this definition:

1. RAPID EXPANSION

When something expands, it spreads out. The term "rapid expansion" means that something spreads out very, very quickly. Speed is the essence of this one!

2. VIOLENT RELEASE OF ENERGY

As something explodes, it releases energy—a lot of it and in a supercharged way. For example, some explosions release giant fireballs or huge, super-tall gas clouds. Talk about destructive power!

WHAT ARE THE EFFECTS OF AN EXPLOSION?

Most explosions release energy as a burst of heat, light, and sound. They can also create **shock waves.** To understand what a shock wave is, imagine dropping a pebble into a still pond. Little waves spread out in circles from the spot where the pebble struck. Energy from an explosion travels in exactly the same way, although you can't see it.

As explosive shock waves move, they push hard against the air—sort of like waves slamming into a brick wall. This impact causes an immediate rise in the temperature, **pressure,** and thickness of the air. In other words, it creates heat and wind.

WHAT CAUSES AN EXPLOSION?

Lots of things! A spark or high heat can cause some materials to easily catch fire, and when they do, the result can be explosive. Certain chemicals when mixed together also react explosively, releasing a rush of gases and flames. Explosions can also happen anytime pressure builds up inside an enclosed space, like inside a volcano. When the pressure gets too great . . .

KABOOM!

EXPERIMENTS THAT
POP!

MAKE SOME NOISE!

Get the party started with these experiments that go POP!

What makes the POP or other explosive sounds? It's those shock waves we talked about. They enter your ears and hit your eardrums hard. Your brain interprets the impact as a loud noise.

In the following experiments, the shock waves come from rapidly expanding air. Let's head to the lab!

BAG BUSTER TIME

If you've ever popped a balloon, you know just how loud of a sound it can make. Let's try blowing up some common household objects, and then smash them to find out which makes the biggest

WHAT YOU NEED

* Small paper bag (lunch size)
* Small sealable plastic sandwich bag
* Plastic shopping bag

PLAY IT SAFE
• Wear your safety glasses

WHAT YOU DO

1. With one hand, squeeze the top of the paper bag almost closed until only a small opening remains.

2. Blow into the opening to inflate the bag. Then squeeze the top of the bag firmly to completely close the opening.

3. Holding the bag in one hand, open your arms wide. Then bring them together hard, clapping the bag between your hands. **BOOM!**

4. Now, repeat steps one through three with the sandwich bag and the shopping bag. What do you hear each time? Number the objects you popped in the chart from softest (1) to loudest (3).

MY RESULTS

Objects	Softest to Loudest (1 to 3)
Paper bag	
Small sandwich bag	
Plastic shopping bag	

HOW IT WORKS

Air molecules push against everything they touch. This force is called air pressure. Because the air inside an inflated object is squeezed into a tight space, it has a greater air pressure than the air outside. When the object bursts, the high-pressure air rushes outward. That change in pressure creates a shock wave that travels to your ears as a loud **POP!** The higher the pressure inside the inflated object, the louder the sound you hear.

POTATO POPPER

WHAT YOU NEED

* Empty, small plastic water bottle
* Freezer
* Fresh potato or apple
* Tape measure

Get ready for some high-flying fun! In this experiment you'll launch a projectile into the air with a deafening BOOM! What's going to help you send the object soaring skyward? An explosion, of course! Prepare for takeoff!

WHAT YOU DO

1. Put the bottle (lid off) into the freezer and leave it there for about 10 minutes.

10 minutes

2. Ask an adult to carve a plug from a potato or an apple. The plug should taper so that it is slightly narrower than the bottle's mouth at one end and slightly wider than the bottle's mouth at the other end.

⚠ PLAY IT SAFE

• Adult helper
• Wear your safety glasses
• Do outside

3. Remove the bottle from the freezer and stick the plug's narrow end in far enough to create an airtight seal, but not so much that the plug is stuck forever.

4. Take the bottle outside and set it in a warm spot. Make sure the bottle's mouth is not pointing at anyone or at any breakable objects.

5. Now step back and wait. Watch and listen for the POP-tacular results! Measure how far away your plug landed from the launcher. Try the experiment two more times to see if the distance changes.

HOW IT WORKS

Air molecules are moving around all the time. When they heat up, they move faster and spread out. But when they cool down, they move slower and press closer together. By chilling the bottle in the freezer, you cool the air inside the bottle and cause the air molecules to squeeze closer. As the bottle warms up, the air inside heats up and expands. After a while, it expands so much that it shoves the plug right out of the bottle! The air escapes. **POP!**

AIR CANNON

WHAT YOU NEED

* Cardboard oatmeal canister, empty, with lid removed
* Sturdy plastic bag, large enough to cover the canister's mouth
* Rubber band
* Paper
* Tape
* Scissors

Cannons have been used for hundreds of years to blast whatever stands in the way. You can build a cannon right in your explosion lab. It launches harmless balls of air at a target with a satisfying **BOOM!**

Ready, aim, fire!

WHAT YOU DO

1. Ask an adult to cut a 2 in. (5 cm)-wide hole in the center of the container's cardboard bottom.

2. Cut a piece of plastic bag large enough to completely cover the open end of the container. Use a rubber band to secure the bag. Make sure the plastic is as tightly stretched as possible across the opening.

3. Cut a thin strip of paper 5 in. (12.5 cm) tall. Fold the strip about 1 in. (2.5 cm) from the end. Tape the folded piece to a flat surface so the rest of the paper sticks straight up.

4. Holding the cannon a few inches (cm) from the strip, aim the end with the hole toward the paper. Give the plastic-covered end a sharp smack with one hand. Did the paper move?

HOW IT WORKS

When you smack the plastic, you cause it to vibrate. These vibrations create the noise you hear in the form of invisible sound waves. The waves travel through the container, pushing against the air molecules inside and causing them to move, too. The air is forced out of the small hole at the end of the canister. That concentrates the air into a powerful burst aimed right at the paper strip. When the blast hits the paper, it wobbles. **Nice shot!**

EXPERIMENTS THAT FIZZ!

Roll up your sleeves.

It's time to get messy! Let's try out some bubbly explosions!

Bubbles are fun—and very scientific. How? An explosion often releases an eruption of gases in every direction. Some wind up as fizz and some as foam.

Most of the fizz and foam in this section comes from a simple chemical reaction. This reaction involves mixing substances called acids and bases. When they come into contact, they react and release carbon dioxide. This gas can do many interesting things. Get ready for some bubbly action!

BUBBLE BURST

WHAT YOU NEED

* Bathroom or kitchen sink
* ½ c (125 ml) baking soda
* 1 c (250 ml) vinegar
* Bubble solution
* Bubble wand

When you blow a soap bubble, it drifts through the air. It eventually lands and bursts with a **POP**. But there's a way to make bubbles that hover in one place!

WHAT YOU DO

1. Close the sink's drain or cover it with a stopper. Dump the baking soda into the sink.

2. Pour the vinegar onto the baking soda. **WHOA!** The liquid erupts into a flurry of fizz!

3. After the fizzing dies down, use the bubble solution and wand to blow a bunch of small bubbles over the sink. Keep blowing until some bubbles fall into the sink. **HEY!** They're stopping in midair!

HOW IT WORKS

Vinegar is an acid and baking soda is a base. These substances react to form carbon dioxide gas. This gas has a greater density than air. The heavier gas stays in the sink instead of escaping upward. The bubbles you blow are denser than air, too. So they sink when you first blow them. But they aren't as dense as carbon dioxide. When the bubbles hit the carbon dioxide layer in the sink, they float like little round ships on a sea of gas.

WHAT YOU NEED

* Reactor tube and base
* 1 packet of dry yeast
* Warm water
* Sugar
* Small balloon (water balloon size)
* Ruler

Instead of blowing up a balloon the old-fashioned way (with your lungs) get help from some invisible friends. Who are they?

Microscopic critters!

WHAT YOU DO

1. Put just enough sugar into the reactor to reach about halfway to the 1 ml line. Then add yeast to the 1.5 ml line and warm (not hot) water to the 5 ml line.

2. Cover the reactor's opening with your thumb. Shake well to mix everything together.

3. Place the reactor in the base.

4. Set the reactor in a warm spot. An amazing reaction will begin that inflates the balloon! Measure the diameter of the balloon every 5 minutes for 20 minutes. Record your results in the chart.

MY RESULTS

Time	Balloon's Diameter
5 minutes	
10 minutes	
15 minutes	
20 minutes	

HOW IT WORKS

Yeast is a type of microbe. It can be dried and packaged so the microbes remain inactive. That is . . . until you add water and bring them back to life. When the organisms wake up, they are hungry and start eating the sugar you added to the reactor. As they chow down, they produce gas as waste. Because the balloon is sealing the tube, the gas can't escape into the air. Instead it rushes into the balloon and fills it up, just as if you were blowing into it! The more gas the yeast makes, the more the balloon expands.

GROOVY LAMP

WHAT YOU NEED

* Reactor tube
* Water
* Vegetable oil
* Red food coloring
* Fizzy antacid tablet (like Alka-Seltzer™)

Oh no! An eruption is about to happen. But you don't need to take cover. The lava you're going to make in this experiment isn't dangerous. In fact, it's pretty GROOVY! A cool and **bubbly** **Lava lamp!**

WHAT YOU DO

1. Fill the reactor tube to the 1 ml mark with water.

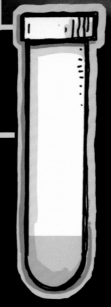

PLAY IT SAFE

* Adult helper
* Wear your safety glasses
* Messy

2. Put two drops of red food coloring into the reactor tube.

3. Fill the rest of the reactor tube with vegetable oil, to the 5 ml mark.

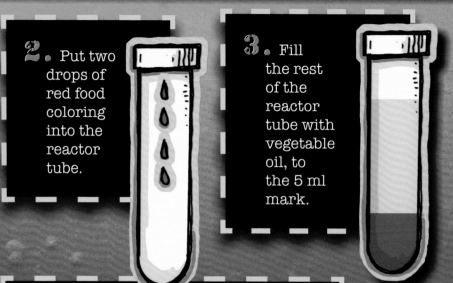

4. Ask an adult to break the antacid tablet into one small piece. Have them drop the pieces into the reactor tube. The lava starts moving!

HOW IT WORKS

Antacid tablets contain an acid and a base. These substances can't combine when they are dry. When they get wet, though—watch out! As water dissolves the tablet, the acid and base interact. That starts the chemical reaction that releases carbon dioxide gas. The bubbles rise to the surface, through the oil, carrying blobs of red water with them. When the bubbles burst, the water sinks beneath the oil again. Why does the water sink?

You'll find out in the next activity!

MAGIC COLORS

WHAT YOU NEED

* Reactor tube
* Light corn syrup
* Red food coloring
* Baking soda
* Water
* Vegetable oil
* Small bowl
* Vinegar
* Blue food coloring
* Dropper

Time for a magic trick! Make layers of liquids mysteriously float on top of one another. By adding some fizz action, you can transform the mixture's crazy, cool colors from red and blue to purple!

WHAT YOU DO

1. Drip corn syrup into the test tube up to the 1 ml mark. Add one drop of red food coloring. Use a straw or another long, thin item to mix.

2. Sprinkle a little bit of baking soda on top of the corn syrup.

3. Tilt the reactor tube. Gently drip water down the side of the reactor tube until it reaches the 2 ml mark.

PLAY IT SAFE
• Messy

4. Tilt the reactor tube. Gently drip vegetable oil down the side of the reactor tube until it reaches the 3 ml mark.

5. In a small bowl, mix a little bit of vinegar with one or two drops of blue food coloring.

6. Gently pour about 1 ml of vinegar on top of the mixture in the cup. Observe what happens.

7. Use a dropper to suck up more vinegar. Poke the dropper into the bottom of the reactor tube so the tip is near the baking soda. Squeeze out a little vinegar. Then, **WATCH OUT** for the **FIZZ!** Keep adding vinegar mixture to the bottom of the cup to keep the fizzy action going.

HOW IT WORKS

This experiment deals with density. Less-dense liquids float on top of denser ones—oil on top of water, on top of corn syrup. When you add vinegar, droplets pile up between the oil and water. That's because its density is somewhere in between that of the oil and water. Then, when you dropped vinegar near the baking soda, the acid and base reacted, causing the entire mixture to froth and its colors to mix. The red corn syrup combines with the blue vinegar to make purple foam!

KABOOM!

WHAT YOU NEED

* Paper towel
* Scissors
* 1 ½ tbsp (25 ml) baking soda
* ½ c (125 ml) vinegar
* ¼ c (60 ml) warm water
* Large cup
* Sealable plastic sandwich bag
* Boom button (from your kit)

When explosion experts need to get rid of an old building, they just push a button and KABOOM! Walls crumble and glass shatters. When the dust clears, nothing is left but a pile of rubble. Try this experiment to set off your own mini explosion. You'll be amazed at what you can blow up with nothing but the power of fizz!

WHAT YOU DO

1. Cut a paper towel into a square that measures about 5 in. by 5 in. (12 cm x 12 cm). Put the baking soda in the center of the square, and then fold the paper towel over the pile of baking soda to create a little pouch. This is your "time-release packet."

2. Pour the vinegar and warm water into the large cup. Then pour the mixture into the plastic bag.

3. Get your helper to quickly place the "time-release packet" into the plastic bag and zip the top closed. **HURRY**, time is ticking!

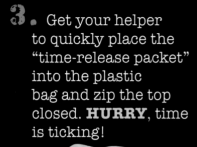

4. Shake the bag up and place it on the ground outside. Step back and watch the explosive show!

HOW IT WORKS

Think back to the Bubble Burst. Remember what happened when you mixed vinegar and baking soda together? The same thing happens in this experiment. As more and more carbon dioxide gas builds up inside the bag, the pressure inside increases as well. At some point, the bag isn't strong enough to hold it all in. It just has to **POP!**

EXPERIMENTS THAT EXPLODE!

Now you're going to go extreme and make things really EXPLODE!

Brace yourself, because this is going to be a real BLAST!

Remember that an explosion has two parts: a rapid expansion and a violent release of energy. You've conducted experiments where you saw these two things happen in a dramatic way—sending projectiles flying, making bags burst, and spraying foam.

How will this section be different? You're going to speed up the reactions, increase the pressures, and make the results even more explosive.

UNDERWATER FIREWORKS

Time to create a BANG! These colorful explosions look just like a dazzling fireworks display. But there's a twist. These fireworks burst not in the air, but underwater.

WHAT YOU NEED

* Reactor tube and base
* Water
* Red and blue food coloring
* 4 ml vegetable oil
* Small bowl
* Cup

WHAT YOU DO

1. Fill a clear cup with water.

PLAY IT SAFE

2. Add the oil and a few drops of each food coloring to the reactor tube and mix.

3. Remove the reactor tube from the base. Gently drip the mixture over the bowl into the water. Droplets of food coloring sink and...

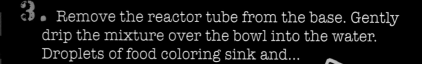

EXPLODE!

HOW IT WORKS

When you drop food coloring into water, the color spreads almost immediately and mixes with the water. This is called diffusion. Oil and water, on the other hand, don't mix at all. By stirring together the food coloring and oil before dropping them into the water, you give droplets of food coloring a waterproof coating. The droplets eventually burst, releasing an explosion of colors, just like real fireworks.

FROZEN EXPLOSION

WHAT YOU NEED

* 20 oz (591 ml) bottle of soda
* Refrigerator
* Large bowl
* Ice
* Water
* 2 c (500 ml) of salt

Explosions are over in a matter of seconds. But this experiment lets you see what an explosion might look like "frozen" in time! Get ready for an **icy** surprise.

WHAT YOU DO

1. Put the bottle full of soda in the refrigerator.

2. After three hours, fill a large bowl with ice and a little water. Sprinkle in two cups of salt.

PLAY IT SAFE
• Messy

30

3. Place the bottle into the ice water for 10 minutes.

10 minutes

4. When time's up, hold the bottle over a sink or go outside.

5. Slowly twist off the bottle's cap. Watch as the LIQUID transforms to ICE!

HOW IT WORKS

Soda gets its fizz from our old friend carbon dioxide. The gas does more than make drinks bubbly, though. It also lowers the drink's freezing point. That causes soda to freeze at a colder temperature than plain water. When you open the super-chilled bottle, you hear the **WHOOSH** of carbon dioxide escaping. As the gas bursts out, the temperature at which the soda turns into a solid rises. **TADA!** The explosion instantly freezes.

SUPER SOAKER

Want a water fight that's truly a **BLAST**? Forget water balloons. Build a device that shoots out an explosive jet of water that will soak everything in sight.

WHAT YOU NEED

* 2-liter soda bottle
* Balloon
* Water
* Nail

WHAT YOU DO

1. Have an adult help poke a hole with the nail into the side of the plastic bottle near its base.

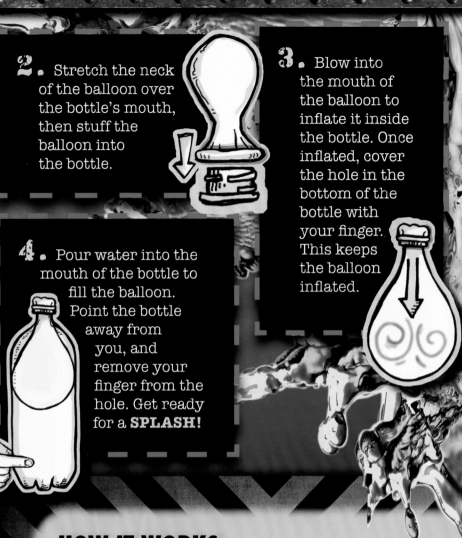

2. Stretch the neck of the balloon over the bottle's mouth, then stuff the balloon into the bottle.

3. Blow into the mouth of the balloon to inflate it inside the bottle. Once inflated, cover the hole in the bottom of the bottle with your finger. This keeps the balloon inflated.

4. Pour water into the mouth of the bottle to fill the balloon. Point the bottle away from you, and remove your finger from the hole. Get ready for a **SPLASH!**

HOW IT WORKS

As you inflate the balloon, air molecules in the bottle are pushed out of the hole. This creates a vacuum inside the bottle. That's the reason why, when you cover the hole with your finger, the balloon stays inflated. Remove your finger, and air flows back into the bottle. This air rushing into the bottle forces the water in the balloon up and out the bottle's narrow mouth. **SPLOOSH!**

JUICE ROCKET

WHAT YOU NEED

* 1 tbsp (15 ml) baking soda
* 1 square of toilet paper
* ½ c (125 ml) lemon juice
* 1 c (250 ml) water
* Empty, small plastic water bottle
* Cork that fits snugly into the opening of the water bottle
* Markers, tape, glue, and paper to decorate your rocket

This project is really out of this world! You're going to send a rocket soaring high into the sky. Prepare for countdown:

three, two, one . . .

BLAST OFF!

PLAY IT SAFE

* Adult helper
* Wear your safety glasses
* Messy: do outside

EXPLODING SCIENCE

WHAT YOU DO

1. Put the baking soda into the center of the toilet paper square. Gather the edges of the square and twist them together to make a small packet.

2. Pour the lemon juice and water into the bottle.

3. Ask an adult to carve a plug from a potato or an apple. The plug should taper so that it is slightly narrower than the bottle's mouth at one end and slightly wider than the bottle's mouth at the other end.

4. Drop the baking soda packet into the bottle and quickly seal it with the plug. Give the bottle a good shake.

5. Set the bottle down on the ground outside. Make sure the cork is pointed away from you, as well as other people and any objects that could be damaged, such as windows.

6. Stand back and wait a few minutes.

LIFTOFF!

HOW IT WORKS

Lemon juice is an acid, just like vinegar. So when it combines with baking soda, a base, the same reaction you first read about on page 17 occurs. The result: a release of carbon dioxide. With the cork blocking the bottle's mouth, the gas has nowhere to go. As the gas builds up inside the bottle, the pressure increases . . . until **POP!** The pressure becomes so great, it blasts the cork sky-high!

LAVA FLOW

Not all volcanoes have violent, fiery eruptions. Sometimes they slowly ooze thick lava instead.

The slow-moving stuff can still be deadly, though. The reason: lava can reach temperatures of more than 2,000° F (1,000° C)! That's scorching HOT! In this experiment, you'll create a gentler, steadier eruption than in the previous projects that will give you plenty of time to see the lava flow!

WHAT YOU NEED

* Ketchup
* Small bowl
* Water
* Dishwashing liquid
* Baking soda
* Reactor tube
* Volcano form (from your kit)

WHAT YOU DO

1. Put a small spoonful of ketchup into the bowl. Add a few drops of water and a small squirt of dishwashing liquid. Stir until everything is mixed well. Pour the ketchup mixture into the reactor tube, to the 2.5 ml mark.

2. Rinse the bowl. Place the reactor tube into the volcano form.

3. Put about ½ tsp. (2.5 g) of baking soda into the bowl. Add ½ tsp. (2.5 ml) of water and stir.

4. Slowly pour the baking soda mixture slowly into the reactor tube that is in the volcano. Swirl the volcano to mix everything together.

5. Stand back and watch the lava flow.

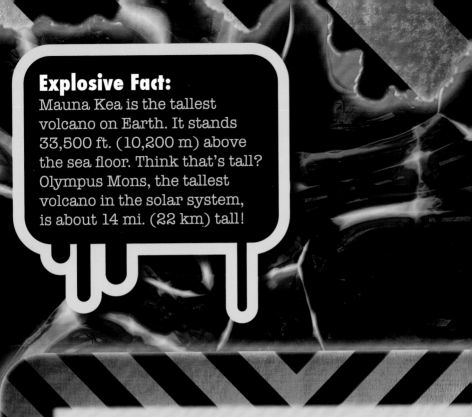

Explosive Fact:
Mauna Kea is the tallest
volcano on Earth. It stands
33,500 ft. (10,200 m) above
the sea floor. Think that's tall?
Olympus Mons, the tallest
volcano in the solar system,
is about 14 mi. (22 km) tall!

HOW IT WORKS

One of the main ingredients in ketchup is vinegar.
It's no surprise that when the vinegar in ketchup
comes in contact with baking soda, it reacts
to produce carbon dioxide—just like in the
previous experiment. This time, though, the acid
isn't full-strength. It's mixed together with the
other ingredients in ketchup, like corn syrup and
tomato paste, which causes the reaction to be less
EXPLOSIVE!

Ketchup also has a high viscosity. The thick condiment
moves sluggishly out of the volcano because it's
about 50,000 times more resistant to flowing than
water. As an added bonus, ketchup's red color makes
your lava look extra realistic!

SODA GEYSER

For this experiment, you'll want to stand back—way back. With the help of some candy bombs, you'll turn a soda bottle into a foaming fountain that shoots

WHAT YOU DO

1. Open the bottle of soda. Place it on a flat surface outside.

⚠️

PLAY IT SAFE

• Messy
• Wear your safety glasses

2. Hold three pieces of candy in one hand and get ready. Before you do the next step, be prepared (very prepared) to

RUN!

3. Quickly drop the candies into the bottle. The soda gushes out of the bottle!

HOW IT WORKS

What makes sodas bubbly? The answer: carbon dioxide. The gas stays dissolved in the soda until something triggers its release. The candies have rough surfaces that attract bubbles of carbon dioxide trapped in the soda. When the candies fell into the bottle, bubbles formed all over them. This triggers the dissolved gas in the soda to burst from the drink. The gas rushed toward the top of the bottle, pushing the liquid ahead of it out of the opening in a giant, exploding geyser!

VOLCANIC ERUPTION

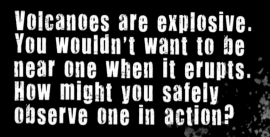

Volcanoes are explosive. You wouldn't want to be near one when it erupts. How might you safely observe one in action?

Build a mini "volcano" and watch it POP its top!

PLAY IT SAFE
• Messy

WHAT YOU NEED

* Volcano form (from your kit)
* Large, shallow pan
* Vinegar
* Dishwashing liquid
* Red food coloring
* Baking soda
* Reactor tube

WHAT YOU DO

1. Carefully fill the reactor tube with vinegar to the 3 ml line. Place the reactor tube into the volcano form. Add a squirt of dishwashing liquid and two drops of red food coloring to the vinegar. Gently mix.

Explosive Fact:
Large volcanic eruptions can send ash into the air, over 17 mi. (30 km) above the earth's surface.

2. Fill the rest of the reactor tube with baking soda. Stand back and watch your volcano **ERUPT!**

HOW IT WORKS

You already know what happens when vinegar and baking soda meet. They make carbon dioxide gas. But what happens when you add soap to the mix? The gas combined with the soap makes tons of bubbles. They blast out of your model volcano in a shower of suds. As long as the reaction keeps going, the lava-like foam keeps flowing.

GLOSSARY

Acid: A chemical compound that gives off positively charged hydrogen ions when dissolved in water. Acids usually have a sour taste

Air pressure: The force of air molecules pushing against a surface

Base: A chemical compound that gives off negatively charged hydroxide ions when dissolved in water. Bases react with acids to form neutral substances

Chemical reaction: When two chemicals interact to form a new substance

Density: The amount of mass in a given unit

Diffusion: The act of material spreading out in a liquid or a gas

Dissolve: To become incorporated into a liquid

Elastomer: Substance with elastic properties made of long, chainlike molecules

Evaporate: To turn from a liquid to a gas

Freezing point: Temperature at which a liquid turns into a solid

Magma: Molten rock found underground

Microbe: Microscopic single-celled or multicellular organism

Molecule: A neutral group of two or more atoms

Non-Newtonian fluid: Substance that has properties of both a liquid and a solid

Pressure: Force applied over an area

Projectile: An object flung or propelled through the air

Shock wave: A disturbance that moves through matter caused by an explosion

Sound wave: Vibrations that travel through the air

Vacuum: Space that doesn't contain any matter

Viscosity: A fluid's resistance to flow